Africa's Struggle to Survive

WARREN J. HALLIBURTON

EDITED BY
KATHILYN SOLOMON PROBOSZ

D1313807

CRESTWOOD HOUSE
NEW YORK

MAXWELL MACMILLAN CANADA
TORONTO

MAXWELL MACMILLAN INTERNATIONAL
NEW YORK OXFORD SINGAPORE SYDNEY

ACKNOWLEDGMENTS

All photos courtesy of Magnum Photos.

Special thanks to Laura Straus for her assistance in putting this project together.

PHOTO CREDITS: COVER: *F. Scianna; Chris Steele-Perkins* 4, 7, 8, 23, 32; *Stuart Franklin* 10, 13, 17, 18, 26, 31; *S. Salgado* 15, 42; *Ian Berry* 20; *Abbas* 24, 28 (bottom), 36; *O. Garros* 28 (top); *Gideon Mendel* 38; *Eve Arnold* 40

Cover design, text design and production: William E. Frost Associates Ltd.

Library of Congress Cataloging-in-Publication Data

Halliburton, Warren J.
    Africa's struggle to survive / by Warren J. Halliburton: edited by Kathilyn Solomon Probosz. — 1st ed.
    p. cm. — (Africa today)
    Summary: Surveys the history and peoples of Africa and discusses the economic, political, and social developments that have arisen as that continent's countries struggle to survive.
    ISBN 0-89686-675-0
    1. Africa—Economic conditions—1960- —Juvenile literature. 2. Africa—Social conditions—1960- —Juvenile literature. 3. Africa—History—1960- —Juvenile literature. 4. Africa-Civilization—Juvenile literature. [1. Africa.] I. Probosz, Kathilyn Solomon. II. Title. III. Series: Africa today
HC800.H35 1993
960—dc20   92-7501

CRESTWOOD HOUSE
MACMILLAN PUBLISHING COMPANY
866 Third Avenue
New York, NY 10022

MAXWELL MACMILLAN CANADA, INC.
1200 Eglinton Avenue East
Suite 200
Don Mills, Ontario M3C 3N1

Macmillan Publishing Company is part of the Maxwell Communication Group of Companies.
First edition
Printed in the United States of America

1   2   3   4   5   6   7   8   9   10

Contents

NOTE: The images in this book are meant to convey visually the spirit of Africa's struggle to survive, and are therefore not captioned. For full descriptions of the photos *see page 45*.

Introduction

In a world where there is an abundance of food, it seems a contradiction that any people should go hungry. Yet in Africa, 20 million children are severely malnourished. One hundred fifty million are underweight.

Within the 52 African nations, 75 percent of the people are afflicted by poverty. In 1992, 14 million children died from sicknesses that could have been avoided by routine treatment at health-care clinics — if only it had been available.

Of the world's 25 million **refugees**, over half are in Africa. These people are forced from their villages or countries because of drought or war. They seek shelter in refugee camps run by relief workers. The camps provide blankets, tents, food and health care. The children who make it to the camps are the lucky ones; many are too weak to survive the long walk to shelter.

The African governments don't have the money to provide their people with enough schools and health-care clinics. The continent's population rate is growing faster than the governments can build schools, faster than farmers can feed people — and the people are suffering.

A brief look at the history of Africa helps one to understand the challenges the continent faces. Up until about the 15th century, the African peoples were a flourishing mosaic of kingdoms, states and communal villages. There were immense empires in Ghana, Ethiopia, Egypt and Zimbabwe and great centers of learning in Timbuktu and Sankore. Highly complex and wealthy states along the coast of East Africa traded with ships as far away as China.

Most Africans lived in communal villages, within their own **ethnic groups.** Ethnic groups are people who are united by common ancestors, language and customs. The Africans worked together to support themselves and welcomed strangers into their homes. Religious and cultural life was important, and the artistic, musical and dance traditions flourished.

The continent was as rich as the people's cultures. Among the abundance of goods were gold and other minerals, spices, all manner of food products, finely woven cloths, bronze sculptures, and intricately designed jewelry.

It was Africa's wealth that made it so attractive to outsiders, mostly whites from European countries like England, Holland, France, Portugal, Spain and Germany. They wanted the continent's wealth for their own nations. The conquest of Africa began with the transatlantic slave trade, starting in the late 1400s.

For four centuries, between ten million and 30 million Africans were forcibly taken from their homelands, and enslaved in foreign nations. Then, the Europeans began taking that which came from Africa itself.

In the late 1800s the **colonialists**, as they were called, invaded Africa. Their guns quickly overcame outmoded African weapons. The huge continent was divided up among the European nations.

The colonial powers forced the Africans to work for them and took the land's mineral and agricultural wealth. Developments were aimed

at increasing European wealth — and did little to improve the people's lives.

The Africans never agreed to domination. They demonstrated, protested and staged rebellions and uprisings. All were brutally stopped by the colonial powers. But the people did not give up. In 1957 Ghana became the first sub-Saharan nation to gain independence. The year 1960 was called Freedom Year because 17 nations were liberated. By 1990 there would be 51 black-majority-ruled nations in Africa. (South Africa remained the sole exception.)

The people of the newly born nations faced many challenges. They had almost no experience in government. Their economies were undeveloped, with industries dependent upon factors they could not control. They were uneducated and had inadequate health-care systems.

The African governments started development programs to improve their economies. They expanded formal schooling. **Literacy**, the ability to read and write, increased. They trained doctors and built medical clinics.

But these steps forward were not enough to overcome the colonial inheritance. Economies began to fail. In many nations, democracy turned into dictatorship. Conflicts between the different ethnic groups arose. Civil unrest grew into wars that rocked the continent. The wars only made the economic problems worse. In many cases, the governments were unable to help the citizens of their nations.

The people began forming development organizations to improve their lives. Today, hundreds of thousands are returning to their traditional roots, adapting them to help develop local industry and successful farming programs. Their voice is becoming a powerful political force. Popular pressure has helped convince governments to start responding to the people's needs. Thirty-one nations have made steps toward democracy. Some have revised their constitutions to balance the powers of government, many have begun allowing opposition political parties, and others have held or plan to hold free elections.

At the same time, there is a trend toward government reform and unity that is sweeping the world. The nations of the world are becoming increasingly interdependent too. In Western Europe, 12 nations united in 1992 to form an economic council. In Eastern Europe, harsh dictatorships were peaceably overthrown. These changes signal that an era of peace, justice, and global cooperation is emerging. Africa, with a quarter of the world's population, cannot help but be a part of this. This is the story of the African people's struggle to survive.

The Farmer's Plight

Zebra, wildebeest and giraffes gather at a stream swollen into a river on the Serengeti Plain. They have eaten their fill of grasses and are now filling their bellies with water. In East Africa this year the rains have come. Farmers have a good chance to fill their families' hungry bellies too.

Most farmers are **smallholders**, which means their farms are five acres or less. Whole families work for long hours in the field to take advantage of the rains. The lucky ones might earn a small profit.

Africa is a continent where 70 percent of the people make their living off the land, and everything depends upon the rains. When they don't come, there is a **drought**. There have been too many droughts in the 20th century for the people to take rain for granted.

Millions have perished from **famine**, or lack of food. Governments have very little food reserves, or surpluses of grains, to feed their peoples in times of trouble. Economies suffer, and so does the land. **Desertification**, or the transformation of fertile land into barren wasteland, has claimed much of the farmland bordering the Sahara Desert.

In 1991, 17 African countries suffered extreme food shortages. Sudan, Ethiopia, Angola, Mozambique, Liberia and Somalia were in the midst of civil unrest, which made their situation even worse.

Hunger causes revolutions. From 1968 to 1974, drought ravaged many countries in Africa. After 200,000 people perished in Ethiopia, the military, under the leadership of Mengistu Haile Mariam, overthrew its emperor, Haile Selassie. Just before the **coup**, he'd been filmed throwing scarce meat to his dogs. Drought hit from 1984 to 1986 and again in 1991. Once more there was war, and Meles Zenawi came to power.

The **nomads** of the Sahara Desert in North Africa have seen their way of life change forever because of droughts. Nomads live in close dependence upon their herds of cattle, sheep, goats, or camels. They migrate, or travel, according to fixed patterns, to provide water and grasses for their livestock.

The herds provide the nomads with meat, milk, skins for clothes and tents, and a means of trade. During the drought of the 1970s, the Moors, Fulani, Tuareg and other nomadic groups located in Mali, Mauritania, Niger and Senegal lost their herds to starvation or thirst. With it they lost their way of life. Many became refugees. Today, thousands still live on the outskirts of major cities where refugee camps once fed them.

The Cash Crop Inheritance

Most African nations are **monoeconomies**, earning most of their income from one **cash crop**. Cash crops are grown for export at a profit. Burundi earns 90 percent of its income from coffee; Gambia earns the same from its peanut crop. Ethiopia and Rwanda get 70 percent of theirs from coffee. In Kenya it's coffee, in Mauritania it's sugar, and in Mali, Ghana and Sudan it's cocoa that earns 50 percent of the nation's income.

The whites introduced cash-crop farming to Africa. Before colonialism, the people were **subsistence farmers**. They planted a variety of crops such as yams, fruits, vegetables, and grains that supported their families and their villages. Farming was communal, and each family worked together to provide for one another.

After independence, the African nations encouraged cash-crop farming. But continuous planting of the same crop without resting the soil sapped it of its nutrients, and yields dropped drastically. In the "peanut basin" of Senegal, the land is "eaten up by the peanut," say the farmers. Here, crop yields are 100 pounds to 200 pounds per hectare (2.47 acres). In areas where the peanut is a new crop, yields are as high as three tons per hectare.

The people are driven to expand their farmlands by the need to survive. In the past, many farmers began working the borderland of the Sahara Desert. Drought came, and the disaster that occurred didn't end with the coming of the rains. The farmers had worked the earth to its limits and, as some say, practically given the land to the Sahara.

Poor land-management practices also cause **deforestation**, or the loss of forest areas. It is increasing at a much faster rate than **reforestation**, or replanting of trees. Out of necessity, the people must cook with twigs and sticks gathered from forests. They open up new land for farming by setting forest fires, and they build their homes from trees they cut down. Their animals overgraze the hills.

Areas of forest the size of Switzerland are disappearing each year. Ethiopia has seen its forested lands drop from 40 percent of the surface area in the early 20th century to three percent today. In Kenya and Burkina Faso, the situation is also critical.

Erosion walks hand in hand with deforestation. In deforested lands, there are no tree roots to anchor the grasses and hold the topsoil in place, and no leaves to break the fall of the rain. Rain doesn't percolate into the soil, it runs off with it. Winds blow fertile topsoil away. Yields are reduced — and farmland becomes wasteland.

Aside from the drop in harvest in many areas of Africa, prices for the farmers' produce have dropped steeply on the world market. But production costs have not changed. In 1960 Ivory Coast needed to sell three tons of bananas to earn enough money to buy one tractor. By the mid-1980s, it cost 20 tons of bananas for the same tractor. And prices for food products are continuing to decline.

The result of this **inflation** is that no matter how much farmers increase their harvest, they won't earn a profit. They are unable to buy seeds, farming tools, or fertilizer, and so they lose their way of life too, becoming dependent on aid from an outside source.

Aid — Help or Hindrance?

Farm and food aid from foreign nations or the government itself often comes with strings attached. Foreign investors can pressure the government to change its policies to get the aid. In turn, the farmers are forced to support government policies that they normally oppose. Many

official programs force farmers to grow crops that are unsuitable for their land, ignoring the people's wisdom about what grows best. When governments give direct food aid to people, the farmers no longer have a market for their own crops. And much of the food aid never even reaches the people who need it. Corrupt officials often sell it to merchants who then sell it in their stores. But maybe the main damage done is that dependence upon an outside source encourages a sense of hopelessness and despair in the people.

Programs That Work

There is an expression that says "Give a man a fish, and he can eat for a day. But teach him how to fish, and he can eat for a lifetime." True aid, many African rural leaders say, is not to throw money or food at the problem but to provide the farmers with the means to produce: Give the credits needed to buy seeds and tools and pay a decent price for the food.

Many organizations have formed to help farmers become self-reliant. **Grass-roots movements**, which spring up from the very soil the people live on, are flourishing. The **Naam groups**, begun by Bernard Lédéa Oeudraogo of Burkina Faso, are one of the more successful programs.

Oeudraogo examined traditional systems of organization of the Mossi peoples, the main ethnic group in the area. He wanted to find one that he would be able to adapt to help the farmers. The Naam social structure of the Mossi suited his purpose. In the Mossi tradition, Naam groups are composed of young people. They teach values like respect for **elders**, provide moral, civic, and technical training for village youth, and encourage cooperative activities and socially useful tasks.

When Oeudraogo first organized the farmers into a Naam-like group, he met with violent opposition — until the villagers and political leaders saw that he was succeeding where they had failed. Farm yields went up, quality of life improved, and so did the people's confidence in themselves and in the future. Today, there are 4,000 Naam groups in Burkina Faso, with 300,000 members.

Naam is not an isolated program. In the border countries of the Sahara, there are over 20,000 rural movements. In Kenya alone, there are approximately 20,000 women's groups. Some, like the Green Belt

movement, founded by Dr. Wangari Maathai of Kenya, focus on refor- estation. Approximately half a million villagers have participated in planting 10 million trees! Food-for-work programs have people build roads, dams and other community improvements in return for food or development aid. Still others form farm cooperatives, build granaries, drill wells, or dig irrigation channels. All rely on traditional communal association and sharing of responsibilities throughout the village.

There are cases where the government works hand in hand with the farmers. In Nigeria the government introduced an import ban on staples like wheat, rice, maize (corn) and barley. Demand for locally grown produce has now increased. There are programs to increase productivity, establish food reserves, **diversify** the crops grown, stabi- lize prices, and address the problem of crop loss due to poor storage facilities or lack of distribution networks.

In Zimbabwe, the government also worked with the people to improve crop yields. Here, civil war was fought for 13 years before black- majority rule became a reality in 1980. They put their resources behind the farmers, supporting them with the basic ingredients: seeds and credits. Instead of telling the farmers how to work their land, they brought in advisors, who gave suggestions about erosion and fertiliza- tion. The production of maize has quadrupled.

Some nations are beginning to pattern their agricultural policies after Zimbabwe's and Nigeria's — and after the successful peasant organizations. They see that significant progress cannot be made without the farmers' willing participation.

The problems Africa faces did not arise overnight and will not disappear immediately. Yet there is enormous potential for wealth in Africa. M. Swaminathan, a farming expert and Green Revolution founder, says that Zimbabwe, Zambia, and Zaire have the capability to produce enough food to feed the entire continent. Even war-torn Ethiopia could become a breadbasket, if its resources were used properly.

The grass-roots movements that embrace African identity, tradi- tions and knowledge and set realistic goals are successful. The growth of these organizations and the cooperation of governments can help the African agricultural potential become reality.

Politics: A Dangerous Subject?

In many African nations, when a person criticizes the government, he or she can be arrested, tortured or even expelled. Politics is a dangerous profession in these nations. Even when a person is not involved in politics but does things that the government doesn't agree with, he or she becomes political.

Many writers have paid a very high price for expressing their thoughts. In Zaire, the playwright Tandundu E. A. Bisikisi was arrested at age 22. He had written a play that ended with these words: "The university is dead, long live the republic! The republic is dead, long live the president! Long live the president!" For that, he was beaten and imprisoned and suspended from his university. The play was **banned** and all copies were seized. One year later he was arrested for a second play. This time, he was released after seven months but took refuge in France.

The political situation is worse in South Africa. Here, the South African Suppression of Communism Act allowed the government to ban people. A person who is banned cannot read, reproduce, print, or publish any speech, writing or statement. Forty-six authors have been banned in this nation. Don Mattera was banned for nine years. During that time he was not allowed to attend any public meetings, and the police monitored his house and his actions.

South Africans live under **apartheid**, a system of laws separating blacks from whites economically, educationally and geographically. Blacks cannot participate in government. While whites live in towns and cities similar to those in the United States, most of the blacks must live in **homelands** such as Lebowa. The 2.8 million people of Lebowa have no running water or electricity — many don't even have roofs over their heads. The settlements are overcrowded, the farmland is over-worked, and there are very few jobs.

The nations of the world have denounced South Africa's apartheid policies and refused to do business with that country. Antigovernment riots and other demonstrations by black South Africans have also increased. South Africa has responded by reforming some of its apartheid policies. In 1990 the government released the South African apartheid fighter Nelson Mandela, who had spent 27 years in prison because of his opposition to his nation's policies. In 1991 the South African Suppression of Communism Act was repealed. It remains to be seen, though, whether democracy will be achieved peacefully or through revolution.

Nor has democracy yet been achieved in many other African nations. The United States evolved over a period of 150 to 200 years into an industrialized democratic nation. It is unlikely that the process will happen in just a few decades in the African nations, especially considering the damage done under four centuries of oppression by Europeans.

Under colonial rule, traditional structures were swept away while the foundations for new ones were never established. People lived under circumstances very much like those in South Africa today. They were not allowed even the most basic of freedoms, like choosing where to live, freedom of speech, the right to vote or otherwise participate in govern-

ment. They were forced to work for very little money on huge planta-
tions owned by white settlers.

The whites imposed artificial borders upon the conquered African
states. For example, the peoples of Somaliland were scattered across
four nations: Djibouti, Ethiopia, Kenya and Somalia.

In Burundi and other nations, one ethnic group was favored over
another. The privileged group received education and training. With
independence, they stepped into leadership roles. In Burundi, the
minority Tutsi peoples, who had been favored during colonialism, took
over. Then the Hutu peoples, who were in the majority, rebelled against
this, the Tutsi responded by brute force — they massacred 200,000
Hutus.

In many nations, the first elections held after independence were
the last. After this, many African governments made detours on the road
to democracy. Leaders cracked down on basic freedoms. With no
watchdogs to alert the people to abuses of political power, many
governments became corrupt. Those in power argued that allowing
opposition parties would enable various ethnic groups to splinter the
nation's unity.

Governmental corruption, coupled with poor economies, created
a climate ripe for revolution. In 1963 the first coup, or military
overthrow of a government, took place in Togo. By 1985 there had been
85 coups in Africa.

The unrest, revolutions and economic problems have led many
governments to realize they cannot rule without consent of the people.
The peoples in many nations have united and are putting pressure on
their governments to liberalize their policies. After the citizens of
Gabon went on strike, the government agreed to allow a multiparty
political system. Strikes and protests forced the governments of Zaire,
Togo, Côte d'Ivoire (or Ivory Coast), and other nations to agree to the
same. Many have also revised their constitutions to become more
democratic. Mali now allows complete freedom of the press.

In Somalia constitutional reforms and a multiparty system came
too late. Rebel unrest toppled the government in 1991. By 1992 the
revolution had turned into full-scale civil war. Anarchy, the absence of

any government, now reigns. The capital city has been destroyed, and so far 20,000 civilians have been killed in the fighting.

In Mozambique one million people were displaced from their lands because of rebel fighting. Liberia and Sudan have also been rocked by long-term warfare. In Liberia the famine caused by dislocation of the farmers was so acute that it led Dorothea Diggs to establish Special Emergency Life Food (SELF) in 1990. With aid provided by the United Nations, SELF distributes food to the 900,000 people affected by the war. In Sudan, Operation Lifeline was set up to help feed the starving children. Nevertheless 260,000 Sudanese were forced to seek refuge in Ethiopia, which is unable to feed its own population.

Yet there is hope. President Meles Zenawi wants democracy for Ethiopia. He says that feudal monarchy and military dictatorship did not work for the country. Yet during the war in which Zenawi came to power, Eritrea, a region in Ethiopia, has **seceded**, or separated, from the nation. And the military still has not been able to bring fighting between the various ethnic groups under control. Industry is virtually nonexistent in Ethiopia, and there is widespread hunger.

President Zenawi is tackling each problem his nation faces. He has met with many of the elders, or leaders, of the rival ethnic groups, seeking their advice and listening to their complaints. He hopes to find a way for the peoples to agree to stop fighting. He is fashioning his own economic plan, which includes keeping the industries in the hands of the government and allowing the peasants to share equally in cultivating the land. He is also planning to allow elections in the country's 12 regions, each of which is home to a different ethnic group, and is ready to accept that the regions will choose independence. Only democracy will unite the people, he says. But what will the people choose? A democracy which will signal the end of a united Ethiopia, instead giving birth to 12 new nations? And will democracy be able to feed the people?

Ethnic Diversity and Division

There are 2,000 ethnic groups and 750 languages in Africa. The Yoruba peoples are great artists. Their bronze sculptures and ceremonial head masks are sought after worldwide. The Tuareg nomadic women compose and sing beautiful ballads about their daily lives. The drums of the Asante call the people together to celebrate the Adae, a festival honoring their ancestors. The Masai undergo elaborate ritual ceremonies when they pass from adolescence to adulthood. The Wodaabe peoples look forward to their annual lineage reunion, in which the men dress in their finest costumes and perform elaborate group dances. The three most beautiful young women in the audience are given the privilege of choosing the best dancer.

These expressions of the people are unique and beautiful. The culture of the ethnic groups are full of spirit, heart and wisdom. Their traditions date back hundreds, sometimes thousands, of years. They sustain and nourish the people more than any amount of money could. And yet, differences between groups are tearing the nations apart at the seams.

In Zaire, there are 50 ethnic groups and 200 languages. Many people of Zaire say their country is a state without a nation. It describes a geographic piece of land, but not the peoples in it. In Kenya, ethnic unrest coupled with scarcity of land has led the Kikuyu to raid Masai landholdings. Lack of common language creates other problems. A literacy worker is sent to a small village to teach the adults to read and write. But he speaks only English; they speak only Kikuyu. A villager goes to the city to make his fortune. Once there, he finds that the businesses will only hire someone who speaks English. All jobs are closed to him.

Situations like these are common across Africa, for in many nations there is one language for business, another for education, and yet another spoken at home. Several nations have made the language of their white rulers the official language, since it is the most "neutral." But is the language of an oppressor really so neutral? And what does it say about the importance of the native African languages? Many people urge a return to their own languages.

— The heart of Africa is in its villages. And its lifeblood is the extended family. Most children live with or close to their grandparents, aunts, uncles and cousins. There are usually six or seven children in each family. The children begin learning tasks from their mothers and fathers from the time they can walk. In turn, the children will take care of their parents in old age. So long as a relative or member of their ethnic group is around, children and elderly will be provided for.

Aside from shared culture, most villagers have a history of shared cooperation. This, more than anything else, has sustained the peoples through their many years of oppression and is now sustaining them through their economic troubles.

In poor nations, the people must do without basic services that other people take for granted. In many African villages there is no

electricity, indoor plumbing, telephones or paved roads. The nearest health-care clinic might be 50 miles away, the nearest elementary school, a seven-mile walk. For most children, high school is only a dream, since most schools are located in the cities.

A typical peasant woman's day in Burkina Faso, and in many other African nations, starts around 4:00 or 5:00 A.M. Her first job is to get water from the nearest well, which can be several miles away. When water is scarce in the area, there are long lines at the well. Some women go to the well in the evening, sleeping overnight so they can be first to draw their water the next morning. The woman collects firewood, cleans the house, pounds the millet for the evening meal, prepares breakfast, works in the fields, returns home in early evening and prepares the meal. Finally, at 10:00 P.M. or so, when her tasks are all finished, she goes to bed. If the woman has an infant, she will carry the baby on her back throughout the day.

The women of Tédy Bâ's village in Senegal walk over 25 miles to market the produce from their cooperative vegetable garden. The walk to the market takes eight hours, and on a good day Tédy Bâ earns $1.60 — the equivalent of two pints of cooking oil. The women run most of the farmer's markets in Africa, in addition to their household duties.

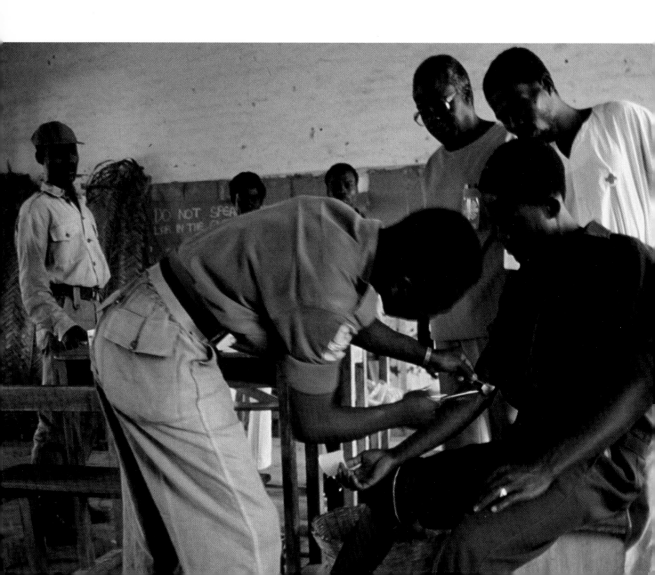

They tackle their jobs courageously and with determination. They know that complaining makes a person bitter, and most go to extraordinary lengths to improve their family's lives.

Economic Puzzles and Progress

Improving the economy is a major challenge facing every African nation. In the aftermath of colonialism, the Europeans took their technology and foreign markets with them. African nations did not have the resources or enough skilled workers to run the few industries that remained. The Africans had to borrow money simply to keep their economies in place. The debts are growing larger with each passing year. In 1986 sub-Saharan Africa received $16 billion in aid, but its debt repayment was another $15 billion.

The African economies are dependent on factors beyond their control. The industrialized nations set prices for mineral resources, such as oil and copper, and for food products, the main exports for most African nations. Prices for these goods have dropped steeply. And with monoeconomies, the governments have no other industry to fall back upon. In Nigeria the main industry was and is oil. During the years when oil was in demand, Nigeria's fortunes rose. But then there was an oil glut in the industrialized nations. And Nigeria's fortunes fell almost as quickly as they had risen.

Many nations are trying to overcome these problems by restructuring their economies. They want to diversify, or spread their export income across many industries. In this way their wealth won't be so affected by drops in the world prices of produce or mineral resources. But diversification will take many years of careful planning.

Debt relief or debt cancellation and an improvement of the international trading environment would help stabilize economies, but this requires the cooperation of industrialized nations.

Many experts say that developing business locally, instead of borrowing more money for large-scale industry, is necessary. The idea is not to throw out Western ways, but rather to merge them with traditional ways.

On the local level, development programs are making it possible for people to start local money-making ventures. The 6-S Association, cofounded by Ouedraogo and the French development specialist Bernard Lecomte, which works with groups of villages, has helped many people help themselves. With funds from 6-S, the AJAC Ziguinchor Federation hired a furniture maker to teach farmers from a village in Senegal to make bamboo furniture. Bamboo grows in many of the rural lands. The farmers learned the trade, returned home, and shared their knowledge with their fellow villagers. They harvested bamboo, and the furniture-making business had begun.

This industry provided the people with a means to make money all year long. Before, their income depended upon the success of the annual harvest. The villagers were able to sell their furniture at a fraction of the cost of commercial products, which made it affordable to people in neighboring towns. And they also paid a percentage of what they earned back to the AJAC Ziguinchor Federation, which could then organize more courses. Today, throughout Senegal, the local furniture industry is thriving.

In Borko, Mali, the 6-S organization taught the village women how to produce soap — a major expense for the people. The soap would be made almost entirely from local materials. Each woman received a loan to fund her business. Many women have not only paid their loans back but have made substantial profits. The Naam and 6-S associations have over a million members. These groups and others, including UNESCO have also helped rural people develop thriving food-processing companies, bakeries, traditional-medicine cooperatives and various craft cooperatives, including weaving. The crafts are finding their market not just in Africa but throughout the world. Income from many of these industries has surpassed income earned from farming.

Each success spurs more development within villages, for the people see that it is possible to improve their lives. And it often spreads to other villages.

In Tanzania the government-created **ujamaa**, or togetherness, villages have built granaries, schools for their children, and health-care clinics and dug wells for clean drinking water. In Burkina Faso a Naam women's group wrote a book on how to organize individual and communal work, make bricks, do the village grinding, and run a day-care center. It also provided information on social, nutritional and economic questions. This book is now helping other rural people start development programs.

On the regional level, neighboring nations are tackling economic troubles by jointly developing industry and integrating their economies. Regional economic communities have been set up in various regions of Africa for this purpose.

Ten southern African nations — Angola, Botswana, Lesotho, Malawi, Mozambique, Swaziland, Tanzania, Zambia, Zimbabwe, and Namibia (which joined in 1990 after gaining independence from South Africa) — are part of the South African Development Coordination Conference (SADCC). The SADCC was founded in 1980 to improve industry, communications and transportation within and among participating countries.

By 1991 the SADCC had established direct air links among most of the nations. Before, the easiest way to get from, say, Mozambique to Angola was to fly to another continent, Europe, and then pick up a connecting flight to Angola. The SADCC has constructed highways between neighboring nations and set up interconnected electric systems. Improved communications systems allow for telephoning and telexing between states, which had been impossible before. New seed variations are tested by the agricultural programs, and an early-warning system for major animal diseases has been instituted. In all, there are 600 projects that are ongoing or have been completed.

On a continentwide level, the Organization of African Unity (OAU) has voted to form an African Economic Community. The OAU hopes this will create economic security and political stability throughout the African continent by the year 2025. The African leaders are optimistic that this will help develop the economies, pay off existing debts, and enable the continent to become self-reliant.

Globalism is about cooperation among nations of the world. The pan-African movement is about cooperation between the nations of Africa. The development movements sweeping through the African rural lands are about cooperation between villagers. And as the grass-roots movements flourish, they might be providing the ingredients for the success of the many nations of Africa: confidence, the ability to control one's destiny and optimism about the future.

Social Structures
and Setbacks

Across Africa, governments have cut spending on health care and education as their economies declined. Many rural health-care clinics have closed down because there is no money to pay for doctors or nurses, and there are severe shortages of drugs and basic medical equipment. In all, less than one-third of the people have access to adequate medical care.

Many needless deaths occur, and serious illnesses that could be cured or prevented with simple remedies go untreated. Each year, almost 150 million people contract **bilharzia**, a sickness that comes from coming in contact with untreated water. Over 440 million people are at risk for bilharzia, the World Health Organization says. These people have no choice but to get their water from a source that is unsafe.

Malaria, carried by mosquitoes, attacks 90 million Africans each year. AIDS is potentially the biggest health problem — already six million men and women are infected with HIV, the virus that leads to

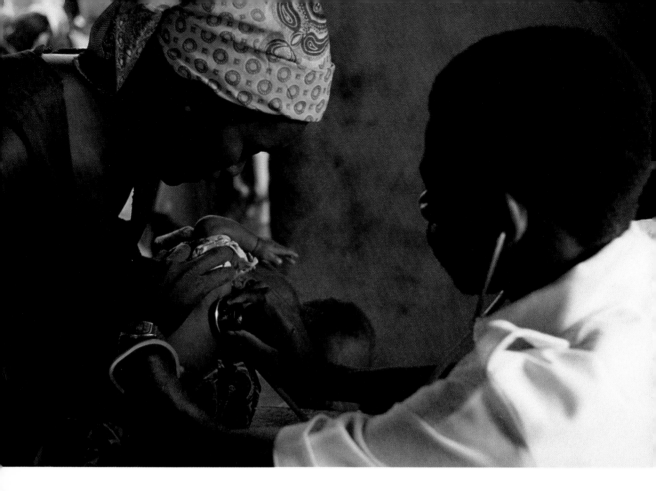

AIDS. Acute respiratory infections and sleeping sickness (carried by the tsetse fly), leprosy and cholera routinely cause severe illness or death. Most of these diseases have been wiped out in industrialized nations.

Africa's need for adequate health-care systems is acute. The continent has the lowest life-expectancy rate in the world — 53 years. Out of every 1,000 babies born in 1992, approximately 100 of them did not live to see their first birthday. (In the United States, the ratio is ten deaths for every 1,000 children born.) One-quarter of the African children under five years old — 29 million — are underweight.

Africa has the highest population-growth rate in the world. Half of its population is under the age of 15. Population growth far exceeds the continent's ability to build schools and health-care systems, not to mention the people's ability to feed themselves. Droughts and political instability only make the situation more critical.

The African peoples are trying many different methods to mend their ailing health-care system. There are traditional healers, but many of their techniques were lost during the colonial years, when healers were harassed and ridiculed. Some were even imprisoned. Healers still live in the rural regions. They are taught medicine by their elders and use successful herbal remedies that rely on the wisdom of their ancestors. Many practice holistic medicine, which means that instead of treating an isolated disease they treat the whole patient, considering his or her emotions and other factors that might contribute to a state of illness.

In the Djinani village of Senegal, pregnant women had to walk many miles on poor paths through forest to get to the health-care clinic to give birth. The women discussed the problem and finally decided to build a village maternity clinic. These women have developed several other community projects as well.

The United Nations Children's Fund (UNICEF) has played an active role in health-care and immunization programs. UNICEF estimates that the lives of about 2.5 million children were saved in 1991 due to an immunization drive. Seventy-one heads of state attended the World Summit for Children meeting of 1990. The goals they set to improve child health by the end of the 1990s included cutting measles deaths by 95 percent, wiping out polio and cutting child deaths by one-third and child malnutrition by one-half.

Governments in Kenya, Tanzania and elsewhere encourage the people to build health-care clinics and have provided support. Naam groups have expanded into the health-care field too. They send villagers to be trained for free in government-run health centers. The workers return to the village with what they have learned, and together the people build a health-care clinic.

The health-care workers' responsibilities don't end in the examining room. Their goal is to prevent disease. They distribute medical kits with certain basic drugs. They provide education on children's nutrition, family planning and how to treat many illnesses. They work with traditional remedies, build latrines for the villagers and teach methods of good hygiene. Health-care workers say the key to success is cooperation, and their goal is community self-reliance.

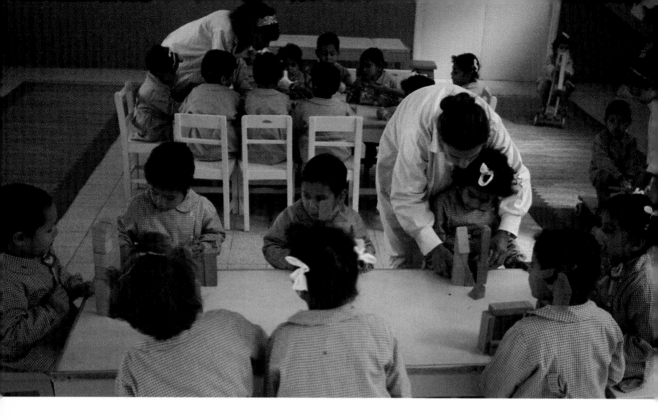

Education

Education is the key to development. For example, to run a business it's necessary to keep records of accounts and clients. To keep track of yearly harvests, it's necessary to keep records. Without an education, it's impossible to write to friends or to read a newspaper, government documents, a child's report card, or the dosage instructions on a bottle of a prescription drug. In 1960, when many of the African nations had begun gaining their independence, only 9 percent of the people were literate, or able to read and write. Under colonialism, the only schools were missionary schools, and they were few and far between.

After independence, newly born nations immediately instituted literacy campaigns. They desperately needed to educate people for business management and technology and government positions that had before been filled by whites. The governments expanded formal schooling, built schools and universities, trained teachers and developed out-of-school courses and vocational training.

Tanzania declared that the government priority for the 1970s was to wipe out illiteracy. They put high school students and retired teachers into service across the country teaching adults to read. They printed books in the many languages of the rural peoples. Today, Tanzania has a 90 percent literacy rate — a farmer is rarely cheated because she or he cannot read or write.

By 1990 the literacy rate across Africa had risen from nine percent to over 40 percent! Follow-up literacy programs include launching newspapers in the many different languages of the people. There are papers in the Shona language in Zimbabwe, in Mandinka and Bambara in Mali, in Zerma and Hausa in Niger and in Swahili in Kenya and Tanzania, to name a few.

Yet the poorest nations of Africa have illiteracy rates much higher than 40 percent. Out of the 14 countries in the world with illiteracy rates of 70 percent or more, ten are in Africa.

Today, failing economies have caused most governments to cut back on educational spending. There still are not enough primary schools for all the children. And as populations continue to grow, it will be increasingly difficult to stamp out illiteracy.

Furthermore, it is simply not possible for many parents to send their children to school. They need them to work in the fields or cannot afford to pay the elementary school fees.

Yet many parents make enormous sacrifices to have at least one child educated. They stretch their limited resources to pay school fees. Usually they choose a boy to go to school, for females are not given equal opportunities in business or in education. Of the 165 million illiterate adults in Africa, 100 million are women.

If a student does well in the standard tests given at the end of elementary school, he will be sent to one of the secondary schools in the towns. If he does well there, he will attend college. Since most African nations suffer from a shortage of skilled workers, it is almost guaranteed that the college graduate will get a job with a secure income.

Education is highly valued among the peoples of Africa. But at present, the gap between those who can read and those who can't might widen.

Inventing the Future

No one questions that the African peoples face enormous challenges as the 20th century comes to a close. Statistics paint a gloomy picture of the future. But they do not tell the whole story. They ignore individual successes and do not take into account the power human beings have when working together toward a realistic goal. And in Africa, a real renewal is taking place.

The power of the people's participation in their own development is opening doors that were once closed to them. The people who believe that they can improve their lives — that drought, famine, and poverty are not inevitable — succeed.

Throughout Africa, more people are persevering and believing in themselves. They are finding their rich heritage a source of strength. Each village that unites to build a granary, bakery, well, or weaving cooperative is investing in the future — their children's future and the future of Africa. Step by step, these villages are walking firmly away from poverty. This is the revolution taking place in Africa today.

Dr. Wangari Maathai, the founder of the Green Belt movement of Kenya, says, "You can see the people being empowered and realizing their self-worth. People realize that change can take place and that it can be spurred by ordinary people with no formal education or sophisticated information at their disposal."

These are the names of just a few of the people's organizations in one small country, Burkina Faso: Unite, Now Is the Time, Let's Trust in God, Parents United, Getting On Well Together, Hope, Hope Resides in Togetherness. With each day, they are growing in number.

In Tintam, Mali, a person said, "The greater the difficulties, the more we will work obstinately." In this village, many people only eat one meal a day — a porridge of leaves and millet. Another said, "Hunger is a teacher that taught us to think."

Development, once it starts and has the will of the people behind it, knows no limits. For example, in just six years, the people in the Manaco region of Mali, in partnership with the 6-S organization, have constructed tracks through the bush between villages, built a training and meeting center and literacy centers, trained village blacksmiths to make various tools, started cattle breeding and fish farming, purchased grain mills and motorized pumps to water the fields, sponsored weaving and soap-making ventures and created a young people's theater group!

And the people are dedicated. In Nombouri, Mali, the entire village built a small dam. Before the dam was built, during the dry season, women had to walk 15 miles to get water. The people, including children, worked from dawn to dusk, not even going home for their meals, until the dam was completed.

When they don't have phones, village organizers must often walk as far as 25 miles to share new developments and ideas with neighboring committees. Other organizers start their days at 3:00 A.M., not falling asleep until late at night — with their pen in hand, at desks, where they are writing developmental reports.

The 2 X F organization has declared that it will wipe out hunger by the year 2000!

The people's voice is indeed powerful. And governments are beginning to acknowledge that in their policies. The leaders of African nations have been taught the hard way — through revolutions, coups, people's strikes and demonstrations — that they cannot rule without the consent of the governed. Many have responded by reforming their governments.

Reform alone, though, cannot pay the debts of the African nations, provide the funds to revitalize major industries, or control prices set for African commodities, or products. The pan-African organizations can help, but there is another source of assistance — that of the industrialized nations of the world — that must also participate.

Many of these nations gained wealth at the expense of their fellow human beings on the African continent. Now it is time to give back. But this time, the solution must not be imposed from outside. Solutions must come from within Africa, and industrialized nations can help by easing or forgiving debts, giving monetary aid, investing privately in businesses, training skilled workers and sending in advisors. But the Africans must be given the freedom to use this aid in their own way. Then the struggle to survive will no longer be a struggle. It will be a story of African success and achievement.

PHOTO IDENTIFICATION _____

(COVER) famine victims wait outside a relief center for aid\Ethiopia; (**4**) refugees at a medical station\Ethiopia; (**7**) refugees from Nigeria\Ghana; (**8**) an undernourished child\Chad; (**10**) planting onion seedlings\Burkina Faso; (**13**) watering crops\Burkina Faso; (**15**) clearing tropical trees\Cameroon; (**17**) gardening\Burkina Faso; (**18**) preparing the ground for planting cabbages\Burkina Faso; (**20**) a white-only area\South Africa; (**23**) a voter registration drive\Namibia; (**24**) civil rights rally\Ghana; (**26**) a flooded street in Khatoum\Sudan; (**28** top) members of the Frolinat party\Chad; (**28** bottom) demonstrations for establishing a native language\Algiers; (**31**) a village without running water\Burkina Faso; (**32**) treating wounded refugees\Ghana; (**36**) a medical school\Algeria; (**38**) a medical clinic\Mozambique; (**40**) a nursing school\Egypt; (**42**) computer training at the University of Yaounde\Cameroon

Glossary

apartheid   A system of laws separating blacks from whites economically, educationally and geographically.

banned   Prohibited.

bilharzia   A sickness that affects those who come in contact with untreated water.

cash crops   Crops that are produced or gathered primarily for profit.

colonialists   A group that exhibits power or control of a dependent area or people.

coup   A sudden, violent takeover of a government by an opposing group.

deforestation   The loss of forest areas due to poor land-management practices.

desertification   The transformation of fertile land into barren wasteland.

diversify   To produce a variety.

drought   A prolonged period of dry weather causing extensive damage to crops or preventing their growth.

elders   Leaders of ethnic groups.

erosion   The process of slow destruction or wearing away of a substance.

ethnic groups   People who are united by common ancestors, language and customs.

famine   An extreme scarcity of food.

grass-roots movements   Organizations formed at the local level, rather than from the centers of political leadership, to bring about change in the area.

homelands   Areas set aside to be a state for people of a particular national, cultural or racial origin.

inflation   An abnormal increase in available currency and credit beyond the proportion of available goods resulting in a continuing rise in the general price level.

literacy   The ability to read and write.

monoeconomies   When governments rely on income from one main industry.

nomads   People who wander from place to place, usually within a well-defined territory.

Naam groups   A grass-roots program set up to help farmers become self-reliant.

reforestation   The action of renewing forest cover by planting seeds or young trees.

refugees   People who flee to a foreign place to escape danger or persecution.

seceded   Withdrawn or separated from an organization, political party or nation.

smallholders   Farmers whose farms are five acres or less.

subsistence farmers   Farmers who produce almost all the goods required by the farm family usually without any significant surplus for sale.

***ujamaa* villages**   Village togetherness created by the government in Tanzania.

Index